About the Author

Born in Holyport, Berkshire in 1940 John Carter attended Ellington Junior School, being the youngest player in the school football team. He fully discovered his sense of humour at Gordon Road secondary school.

Gaining his City and Guilds in response to the college principal's suggestion that he might have a link missing, he worked first as a compositor and later as a private haulier, accumulating anecdotes from 1972 to 2020. An amateur dramatist and judo black belt, in 1967 he married Maureen Connolly, who blessed him with two children, Christopher in 1969 and Eleanor in 1971. He now lives in Burnham, where he is passionate about the countryside and classical music.

Kip's Dream

To Vivien (Steve)
Best Wishes
LOVELY MEMORIES
Love Kip x

FRONT COVER:—
BRIAN MYSELF DEV

John Carter

Kip's Dream

Olympia Publishers
London

www.olympiapublishers.com
OLYMPIA PAPERBACK EDITION

Copyright © John Carter 2023

The right of John Carter to be identified as author of
this work has been asserted in accordance with sections 77 and 78 of
the Copyright, Designs and Patents Act 1988.

All Rights Reserved

No reproduction, copy or transmission of this publication
may be made without written permission.
No paragraph of this publication may be reproduced,
copied or transmitted save with the written permission of the publisher,
or in accordance with the provisions
of the Copyright Act 1956 (as amended).

Any person who commits any unauthorised act in relation to
this publication may be liable to criminal
prosecution and civil claims for damage.

A CIP catalogue record for this title is
available from the British Library.

ISBN: 978-1-80439-201-0

This is a work of creative non-fiction. While events in the titular piece
are loosely based on true recollections, identifying details have been
omitted to protect the privacy of the people involved.

First Published in 2023

Olympia Publishers
Tallis House
2 Tallis Street
London
EC4Y 0AB

Printed in Great Britain

Dedication

To my wife Maureen and my children Christopher and Eleanor. And to the memory of my dear friends, Brian and Dev, whose adventures with me are herein re-imagined.

Acknowledgements

I wish to thank my wife Maureen for typing my handwritten poems with the attendant neurotic changes and adaptations en-route; Chris my son for handling submissions, design and technical details; my daughter Eleanor for her academic appraisal; and Wendy for coping, with good grace, with the countless outbursts of poetic inspiration throughout the creation of *Kip's Dream*.

Outline

This selection of poems includes amusing takes on traditional nursery rhymes, more thought-provoking observational and narrative pieces, a swashbuckling highwayman story and the principle piece, the semi-autobiographical 230 verse epic poem *Kip's Dream*.

Written in the first person and predominantly in the present tense, the latter essentially comprises the dreamt reminiscences of an elderly man recalling events experienced by his nine-year-old self.

Christmas Aftermath

The blissful pend between Boxing Day and New Year's Eve.

At last the Christmas aftermath,
The settled state approaches new year's dawn,
With embryonic resolutions nebulous
Now crystalised and clear.
Wish not away the first bleak months
To want for summer's warmth or spring new born,
But sanctuarise in late December's
Quiet anticipation of the year.

Have You Seen

Have you seen the woods today?
Have you savoured rare delight?
Autumn fragrance – damp and amber – dark and bright,
From season spent to russet hue,
Breathe deeper on ascent now pause to see anew
The undulating cherished place on time's rich unabating face,
Whose darkening course you cannot hold,
Then just delay the tranquil phase
When you will tread a dappled path and leave the woods behind.

Have you seen the woods today?
The precious present passed away.

Salvation

Heaven is striven for, day upon day,
Hell can be one single action away.

Destiny

On reflection, where all past's revealed,
With no intention hid nor deed concealed,
Questioning if destiny is sealed,
Stands the prisoner in an open field.

I Was Not

I was not, and then I was as far as one can tell,
Finite fool in length and breadth and height and time as well.
But if nothingness is all there'll be that's nothing new because
I'll never be not for as long as I was not before I was.
So I'll be not again, or what?
Or was it I was never not?

Or could a past infinity
Arriving at the start of me,
Who then perceives the aeons hence
As never-ending consequence,
A misconception simply be
With its own credibility
Asserting categorically
Something from nothing cannot be,
Unless within the sphere of nowt
Exists potential wanting out?

So was there not before there was? I simply cannot tell.
Unimaginable nowhere with nothing there as well,
It seems to me that what we see's a mystery because
If past infinity can't be, yet nothing never was,
Then trapped in time we've lost the plot,
We'll trust that God is never not.

Imagination Space

Imagine space, not time nor place,
Nothing can it be,
But should a sphere by chance appear
It becomes infinity.
Space you see is just a three-dimensional facility

Or is it four? Could be more,
Immortal one who would be sure.

Evolution

Why stay immersed in salt water
With occasional strife on the sand?
When all you need is a leg and a lung
To live a long life on the land.

Seasonal Shortage

A shortage of holly's quite tiresome this season,
The plants of the red berry type.
Plus a shortage of toms. (when there are some) the reason's
You can't eat the ones that aren't ripe.
And a shortage of kindness in weasels this year,
Who insist upon goading the gnomes,
Waxing mindless in Harrods with seasonal jeer,
From a shortage of "Don'ts" in the homes.

Hence with shortage of thought they'll turn bulbs on and off,
Mum can't see so she won't call a halt,
But their shortage of height means they can't change a light
On the tree should a short be the fault.
Then there's shortage of light in the garden,
Save the pale moon that graces the snow,
But the rush of two torches from under the porch is
Enough to set faces aglow,
Where there's shortage of wood to make structures
(No one's heard of a snowman's camp)
With a shortage of sense they've dismantled the fence
For their snowman's protection from damp.

Truth to tell in December they're restless,
Still we in the face of it might
Do as well to remember it's Christmas
When a shortage of grace must be slight.

Through a shortage of understanding
We'll arrive at a shortage of joy,
True a shortage of careful handling
Leaves a shortage of toys for the boy.
It's not that a shortage of help from the weasels
Is worse than a shortage of logs,
Simply their shortage of effort to please seemed
Unfeasible when they were sprogs.

Now from shortage of message
My verse seems it might have been hitherto veering away
From its course first envisaged,
While themes mightn't quite be the ones it set out to convey:-
Of the Second world's shortage of sought-after solace,
The Third's with food shortages still,
While the West's current shortage of shortage could shortly be shortened by shortage of will,
But the point (with a shortage of time to conclude)
Which in short I had sought to propound,
Is there's never a shortage of short-sighted idiots
At Christmas or all the year round.

Chosen

He wasn't chosen,
Not because he somehow fell from grace,
But more because he didn't have
A 'being chosen' face.

Ellington

(Gender disparity)
"Thank you for telling me, Betty,
From knowing the truth we've all gained,
By telling your tale will good order prevail
With the school's reputation maintained."

Here "Don't tell tales boy" is a matter of course,
As the hand meets the ear with considerable force.

Gordon Road

A benefit of the cane was to convince one of the inadvisable course of being a smart-arse all of the time, and to instill a recognition that a man must accept the consequences of his actions without complaint. Oddly it could serve as a feather in one's cap if so perceived.

Where's ended the laughter:
"I want to see Carter, Classey and Nash after prayers,"
Now anticipate pain as you wait for the cane
At the bottom of Adderson's stairs.

Dry Dock

On hearing that an ocean-going passenger liner in dry dock was to have its funnel converted into a glass-walled restaurant.

I was not built for this,
To be refashioned, gutted, made inert,
My funnel bleached to sedentary purpose,
From that red stack which cleaved the ocean's hail,
Where spray-lashed black
My heaving iron hull withstood the gale
That breathed about my bright-lit bows
To set romantic course,
Through harsh night surf on darkest swells,
The great Atlantic force.

I'd have this limp alternative abate,
And men restore me to my splendid state.

Ambition

On hearing that an elevated position in a mediaeval court was to attend to the king's posterior following his ablutions. I was at a loss to imagine who would want the job.

Straightener of the Portraits was my role for one whole year,
With time expired I was promoted to a higher sphere,
Then creeping sycophantically to please the powers that be
I nailed the job of jester, which had long appealed to me.
And though this role was viewed by some as something of a farce,
I'll not aspire (from no desire) to tend the monarch's arse.

Although prepared to play the fool
I would be spared the privy stool.

Afterthought

I see the King and realise
The danger of his girth's extent.
Footwear of a larger size
Might a forward lurch prevent.

But in the light of recent news
(Having thirty stone surpassed)
He doesn't need the larger shoes,
Counter-balanced by the arse.

Johnny Herbert's Last Race for Jaguar

A Jaguar representative suggested that I write a poem on Johnny Herbert's last race for Jaguar.

Eyes of azure pierce the shield,
The final challenge now in sight,
Where blazing Michael heads the field
Still wary of McLaren's might.

As blood and blade the spearhead four
Who dare not stall nor set to creep,
While back amid the haze and roar
The leaping cat has yet to leap.

There, holding fast in searing heat,
All emerald shrouded (strokes the wheel)
With farewell duty still to meet
Must gentle John display his steel.

All fired, the multicoloured missiles
Stay – the countdown's at an end,
<u>Now</u> the furious torqued projectiles
Scorch the straight and grip the bend.

A visor tilts for Häkkinen,
With gain awry he quests in vain;
Bears down upon blue Benetton
While yellow Jordan's fortunes wane.

The scarlet banner's all but won,
Teutonic nerve must hold the sway,
And half are left when halfway done
From clash and swerve that cost the day.

Where fractions make the dif-fer-ence
Bold Herbert's charge is off the pace;
Maintains his wake, but seconds hence
He'll stare the reaper in the face.

A tendon rips and flips the back,
A prancing twist should miss the wall,
The Jaguar splits and claws the track
But hurtles on in lateral sprawl.

Though Johnny had not sped to die,
And future glory may well be,
It was the cat who said goodbye
On Michael's day of victory.

Almost

Though John's bemoaning the fact he's to shelve
Any notion of owning a Jaguar V12,
Would it transpire, when time even doubles the price,
Could inspire then to rhyme seven syllables twice?

Well, almost!

Mallard

I reflect on Mallard.
Mallard reflects on itself.

In oil aroma, steam and smoke,
Mallard heaves into its stroke
Re-bearinged in metallic flow
Exuding just enough deco

Bereft of valance either side
In lanky red revolving stride
As languid rods of steel rotate
The driving wheels all six feet eight,

And you'll recall that while ago
When your great trial you'd undergo,
And Duddington and Bray would know:
'Just how fast does this engine go?'

And set your streamlined deco brow
Through speed restriction, then as now,
To move into an open sphere
Above Stoke Bank where rails were clear

That bore your measured rhythmic flow
With just six carriages in tow,
'Til came the men and came the hour
When Duddington unleashed the power

That drove blue iron through billowed smoke
For piston strokes to go for broke,
That made the counterweights rotate,
All tonnage to accelerate,

Increased through traction from the power
To reach one hundred miles per hour
Where still within familiar feel
Revolved the oiled and heated steel

All working in respective roles
Responding to the cab's controls
(From swift internal tractioning
To spinning outside valve gearing)

Set by the men in record blast
With heat and vapour racing past,
Their quest, as they would be aware,
Momentous test they couldn't share.

In oil aroma, steam and smoke,
Near raging fire fed by the stoker
Unfamiliar speed was reached
And one hundred and twenty breached.

At one hundred and twenty three
Was shackled task perceived to be
As freedom in a speeding cage
In Mallard's fired and flat-out rage?

To one hundred and twenty-four,
Where steam had been just once before,
Still final torque would not relent
'Til distant short and bearing spent,

And who was privileged to view
That iron profile rush of blue,
Or frantic ticks of pistons heard
Where racing rods and wheels were blurred?

'Til throttled back and clanking rough
Where speed might just have been enough
As heated brakes decelerated
Coaches in inertiad state

All slowing from their race 'til they
Would parallel your pace today,
Now settled in your steady stroke
In oil aroma steam and smoke

As bathed in evening light you glide
With lanky red revolving stride
Now easing to a halt where you
Can rest on rails and laurels too.

Splendid Mallard, blue A4,
Remembering the day when your
Credentials were forever fixed
At one hundred and twenty-six.

Crooked Man

There was a crooked man
Who had a crooked smile,
He only walked a crooked path
And made a crooked pile.

Bo Beep

Little Bo Peep has lost her sheep
And knoweth not whither they wander,
Whether hither or thither they tarry not with her
So dithers she hither to ponder.

Jack Sprat

Jack Sprat, deprived of fat,
Ate precious little lean,
His wife devoured pears, eclairs,
And buns with cream between

A Likely Tale

Sing a song of sixpence and never tell a lie,
Isn't four and twenty birds excessive for a pie?
Black or white or parrots bright
They'd hardly stand and sing
At a hundred and fifty Fahrenheit
Not even for a king.

It's conceivable a counting house
Is where kings count their money
And possibly a parlour's where
A queen would consume honey.
More than likely maids would favour
Gardens to hang clothes
But there's no way a baked blackbird
Would peck off someone's nose!

Simple Simon

Simple Simon met a pie man
Going to the fair,
Said Simple Simon to the pieman
"Sir, are you aware

"That your pies contain preservatives,
Which do, admittedly,
Afford a slender benefit that gives
Your wares longevity?"

"Notwithstanding what I'm able
To have labelled 'salt resource',
Bringing hazards to the table
(Not your fault, of course).

"So prevailing on you chiefly
For your sympathetic ear
I'll make my point quite briefly,
Unequivocally and clear:-

"I shall, in deference to my health,
From pie-purchase abstain,
So suffer not diminished wealth
Should peckishness obtain.

"Eyes that must of your wares take heed
Would doubtless hold the view
That your pies are just the fare folk need
To nourish them anew,

"But my preferred consideration
Leads me to conclude
(Without a word of condemnation)
We need not wax rude,

"That my well-being's 'Simply' expressed
In healthy facial hue
And retention of my penny
Lest financial stress ensue."

Said the pieman unto Simon
"Hold on to your cash,
You're not on the wavelength I'm on,
There's no sense in being rash.

"Though keen to make one pie sale more
That's closed 'tween thee and me,
I'll no advantage take of your
'Supposed' simplicity,

"So let that coin in your tight purse
Remain beyond my reach,
Nor fret my words might sound quite terse,
My pies are four quid each."

Humpty Dumpty

Humpty dumpty sat on the wall
Beneath the looming belfry tall,
High above the rain-soaked earth
Bells to dissonance gave birth,
Discord rang to the heavens black
And an ebony sky began to crack,
Lightning's crooked fingers hung
And driving hail the pale egg stung.

With frenzied arms of meagre strength
And whirling legs, deprived of length,
He reeled revolved and gripped the wall
To rectify lest he should fall
Then leered in dread to the granite bed
And the wild winds wailed for the shells of the dead,
All woven in fugue with the choirs of hell
They bade him make his last farewell
Who whirled and twirled in wild despair,
Who's groping fingers hooked the air,
Who rolled his eyes to the rapid skies
And lurched aloft with hideous cries
To plunge the deathward last descent
And night absorbed the choir's lament.

All the king's horses and all the king's men
Couldn't stomach that again.

But,
Egg mender Ted with his nightmare shed
From the din through the window was quick from his bed,
To alight with a lantern on troublesome course
To the cries in the night and discover their source
Where he'd never take fright at the puddles all red
But would roll the egg right to his workshop instead.

Humpty dumpty's mended now
From a craftsman's hand and a resolute vow,
A happier egg ne'er did fortune befall
And he sits to this day – on a smaller wall.

All traumas of the past long gone,
With health and safety harness on.

Bob the Bore

Having helped Humpty, Bob the Bore could do with support.

Bob the Bore had entered the store,
Was that a cough or a scoff?
When he'd stuck in his oar and proceeded to bore us all rigid
til told to 'sod off'.

Not quite in so many words of course
But the message abundantly clear,
Pained expressions obtained while the boredom remained,
All would rather see Bob from the rear.

Thick skinned though he is Bob was saddened by this
As he exited on his way,
But Claire, being fair, with compassion to spare,
Followed after to brighten his day,

Where she showed him affection so Bob on reflection
Had sweet recollection to keep,
And she listened in awe to some tales that would bore
Less receptive recipients to sleep:-

Of Bob's hamster (the prankster) who'd diced on his wheel
Then impishly darted to hide,
And he told her of summers, collecting bus numbers,
And showed her July's Spotter's Guide.

And now they are wed Bob's emerged from his shed
Where a broken gnome's pending repairs,
And he never looks back as he hangs up his anorak
Pegged at the foot of the stairs.

Claire is there in his arms, without question or qualms,
Bob has rare hidden charms that's for sure,
Where they're free from all strife she's his beautiful wife,
He's the love of her life, Bob the Bore.

Hopper

(Ode to a state of hopelessness
Should a wheel rotate and a hopper hop less)
On finding a grasshopper under my front wheel, I elected to proceed
with compassionate caution.

I hope there's not a car behind, as gently I reverse,
A hopper's life is on the line (or rather on the grass)
Rear vision to the right accords with notions of fair play,
While forward motion might afford a bad start to his day.

Git Talk

While conversing with a friend of mine,
Attempting to shed light,
Analytically deliberating,
Waxing erudite.
A young man (interjecting)
Not intending any slight,
Said "That's Old Git Talk innit?"
We'd a feeling he was right.

Picasso

After viewing a ludicrously priced Picasso sketch in a Petworth antiques centre.

I once misread the price tag
On a small Picasso sketch:
Two-plus million, made an offer all the same.
I concluded from my lesser bid
It seems a lot, two hundred quid,
Still, I guess the value's in the frame.

It's clear a oner's nearer the amount the sketch should fetch,
It's something of a bosk-up after all.
Oh well, when someone's tried it's really sad
But when a picture's quite that bad
You wouldn't want it hanging on your wall.

Tilly

I'd left my mobile phone in a friend's car. I phoned from my landline to locate its whereabouts. Tilly, his eleven-year-old daughter answered jokingly demanding a reward. I determined that her reward would be a short poem saying she would be the last person to even dream of asking for one. When the full facts were revealed, they merited a poem depicting her father Ashley as a grasping miser, Tilly an angelic child and painting myself in an absurdly heroic light.

Hats off to Tilly, she alone
Went forth to find my Nokia phone.
My solace seeking to afford,
That dear child asked for no reward.

For her all satisfaction's found
In helping others, there's no sound
From her of greed or avarice,
In simply giving she finds bliss.

And should I broach reward of coin
She'd find it hard her disappoint-
ment to disguise in her sweet face
(My vulgar tip so out of place).

So for her selfless attitude,
A poem to show my gratitude.

Prior to my giving Tilly's gift
There'd been a father/daughter rift
When from a darkened corner he
Had urged the child to claim a fee.

Then tears had welled in Tilly's eyes,
In disbelief and stunned surprise
The girl stood trembling there where she'd
Just heard the voice of wanton greed.

And worse was yet to come when he
Would add insult to injury:
"You've just found J.C's phone so why
Don't you now bleed the bastard dry?"

"Oh Father dear you've taken leave
Of all compassion, I believe
If that great man my phone had found
He'd want no 'bung' to bring it round."

She'd learnt that ghastly term of late
From one who now spoke words of hate:
"He needs that phone, make no mistake,
Can't you for once be on the take?"

"No sir, I could not possibly,
None are so noble as J.C,
Whose heart is full of charity,
Whose face exudes integrity.

"Have you not seen, when others cave,
He takes the helm to ride the wave,
Then from the cheers of gratitude
Retires in modest solitude.

"He needs no medals, seeks no praise,
Indeed he would himself erase
From records penned or honours boards
For other men to move towards
The glory that the boastful crave
Who wax more shrill yet are less brave
With ego cups filled to the brim
While wishing they could be like him.

"No ransom sir from one who'd seek
To guide the proud and help the weak.
Can't we repay in measure small
The joy that he affords us all?"

"What joy? When he can gloat to see
My own inferiority.
You cannot know the pain, the sting,
With him so good at everything.
We've lost while you play caring kid,
You've cost us upwards of a quid."

Too mean to light the darkened room,
He peered out from the corner's gloom,
And then recoiled with fingers thin
To draw his knee towards his chin,
And in one final spasm he
Broke down remorseful on one knee.

"Oh Tilly dear, I've been so wrong,
You're right in all you've said, and long
May we stay friends with one who lives
For others, and who only gives."

Self One

During a house removal I struck my head on a protruding object. Tiny Tim my helper observed, "You'll do anything to draw attention to yourself, JC!" Mirth all round which merited another poem on self-obsessed absurdity.

A question that I'm being asked
With increased frequency,
By scores of folk who understand -
Ably look up to me,
Is a point that must be settled,
Can't just be left on the shelf,
It's a question filled with interest:
How would I describe myself?

When the line receiving talent
Stretched from genius to runt,
I think it's fair to say that I was
Pretty near the front,
The first half dozen possibly
It's difficult to say
Simply judging from achievements
Or the clever things I say

I'm so f***ing good at everything
But having said all that
You're pressing me to summarize
I'd say I'm where it's at.

Self Two

In ridiculous like vein.
Apart from exceptional genius
And command of spoken word,
With inappropriate modesty
Bordering on the absurd

God's gift to me was humour
And you'll never know the half,
But I wish when I'm trying to be sensible
The blighters wouldn't laugh.

The Bechstein

The place where stands the Bechstein grand's
Raised by its presence there,
For listeners, singers and performers
Music's joys to share.
Where in that hallowed parlour,
When other sounds have ceased,
The Hammerklavier Sonata
Waits to be released.

A Northern Tribute

Amadeus Mozart,
Wolfgang to th's chums,
Amazed by thy melodic art,
Our gang'll raise us thumbs.

Long Will

In the early 1960s my friend suggested that we each write a short story on a highway robber who encounters a life-changing vision. A few weeks later, in his country cottage, a rescued baby fox sat in one corner of the room with the cat eyeing it suspiciously from the opposite corner. John's wife Jackie crocheted by a log fire while we paced the room in turn reading aloud our contributions (shortcomings with both, but good fun).

By moorland fern the buckles glide,
He narrows time with rapid stride.
Dark auburn locks a cloak enhance,
And vigilance dictates his glance.

Though scarlet weave the cloak enrich,
Check patches to his britches stitched,
Some moral compass might deny,
And so his actions justify.

So quickens he the steadfast pace,
Some further distance to displace,
Strides paths whose inconsistent wend
Mere hindrance to his motives lend.

And blustered trees in writhing form
Bow slender arms to the coming storm,
While all about first glints of rain
Seek to soften earth's harder plain.

Where yet the quest is set to last
(Recalled the shadows of the past)
That clouded longed-for joy before
Where heavens frowned upon the poor.

Now Will's objectives clearly set
On conquest must be duly met,
To seize the gentry's hefty purse,
To jest when they his blatance curse.

Apt are his dwellings on the prize,
For now the road before him lies,
All haste must quench the fire within
Will's heart if he the day should win.

Now time, once short lies there to kill,
Before it cripples mind and will,
He darts to shadow's safe confines,
In shrub his wretched form reclines.

Oft oak and stealth-protecting glade
Have known the hazards of his trade,
Now seek their comforts to disguise
The horrors of his enterprise.

In lingering dwells he on a kinder place,
Wherein nature's favours to embrace
Allows imagination hold the sway,
To drift in paths of fancy where it may.

Sees moors where soft terrain supports the dew,
In endless seeping plains of pallid hue,
Thatch dwellings rest where slender spires climb,
(His reminiscence of a former time)
He deeper drinks of recollection's wine.

Soft rain still patters on the leaves,
Frustration tells of soaking sleeves,
Long pistols at the ready checked,
Composure by the visions kept.

Scarce audible at first by distance kept,
Faint sounds his senses touch on breezes swept,
And mingled, varied noises draw more near,
Momentum permeates the atmosphere.

In slow crescendo, hooves and horns and wheels
Their unrelenting course more distance steals.
Will's trembling fingers trace his furrowed brow,
The quest be lost should courage fail him now.

He leaps and scrambles to the fight,
Raised guns reflect the turquoise light,
That coachman topples in the fray,
Whose wit has known a sharper day.

Will's look is fixed, his mind is set,
The traveller's pleas are harshly met,
He stands aloof and makes demands,
Fear bids them heed the grim commands.

Short lived the collar's heat, the passions blind,
Soon yield themselves to calmer frames of mind.
As now Will's sense of decency's on trial
When ladies, courting favour, deign to smile.

Still having condescension (for a price)
He makes a joke their pleasure to entice,
A witless jest (observed in retrospect)
None ever further from desired effect.
Still caution reigns lest manners seal
The fate of limbs that gallows feel.
The quest soon o'er, the deed near done,
Gold coins and silver almost won,
He backs away but keeps awake
To the consequence of one mistake,
Then turns and flees for freedom's sake.

Sporadic birch receives his stalking flight,
With bat-like countenance he treads the night,
To leave the road a hundred oaks behind,
To favour woods where narrow pathways wind.

To choose familiar trails oft trod before,
To pace the rapid clouds where pine trees soar,
To hear the wild owl sound his wafting note
(nocturnal sage, ill blessed with morbid throat).

Will hears the night's foul chorus at his ears,
And oft succumbs to superstitious fears,
Remembering dark tales his father'd tell
Of woodland's bracken pits where goblins dwell.

Beyond the place where towering poplars loom,
Some shorter growths his whereabouts entomb,
Vexed, notched encroachments o'er him seem to leer,
As twisted, grinning dwarfs those clumps appear.

In sudden silence hangs the unknown place,
A rancid scent of death all sounds replace.
By what strange force is reason intertwined
With subtle trance, or logic undermined?

What mirage does the gaze perplex,
Should hell some trembling mortal vex,
With spirits grim of slight restraint
When terror's purpose stands to gain?

The robber scans all shadows stark,
None move save one between the bark,
Be ghost or mortal, friend or foe,
Never did Will more terror know.

Was ever ghost so keen of glance?
Made half as tall by crooked stance.
Was ever cheek more pale and drawn,
Were fingers e're so spent of brawn?
Did larynx ever poignance lend,
As that Will's ears scarce comprehend?

"Art thou the robber lately from a raid?
If it be so this fair one pleads thine aid."
Will stares bemused as in some awful dream,
Beholds the gentle subject of his theme:

In perfect realisation of her kind,
A child (by nature's miracle defined),
Ill-clad in rags that poverty impart,
Fear-drained compassion tears Will's English heart.

He bids her guardian tell (in mercy's name)
From whence, by what misfortune this child came.
To flinch as light and thunder tear the sky,
Then cloaked in darkness hears the ghost's reply:
"This tiny victim of events,
Her poor dead father now laments,
His only crime was that of thine,
Yet had he not thy wits' incline.

"Nor favoured e'er did fortune's hand
Twixt men and misadventure stand,
On first encounter cruelly bled
Of bounty, thence to gallows led.

"He hangs this hour while infants grieve,
And ever more, save one reprieve,
That by some chance a worthless knave
Commit himself to that lofty grave."

He sways who scarce believes a keenest ear,
From whence they came the strange pair disappear,
To destination far beyond recall,
Bewilderment's prize lad to stand or fall.

All creatures stir that sense protection's wane,
The impending storm no longer bears restraint,
As thunder's daughters vex the rooted freaks,
A driving tempest through the forest shrieks.

Trees lurch and toss with many a nuance wail
With towering backs that arch before the gale.
The moaning sap-veined lords proud protest make,
To roar with sodden claw to bow or break.

For many an hour Will strides confusion's course,
And many a trail declines reveal its source.
'Til when subsidence lends the stars their right,
His eyes rejoice to view a dwelling's light.

His faltering steps the slope negotiate,
In crippling heat, tired heavy lungs pulsate.
Still keeps the swimming house before his gaze,
Until the creaking lantern o'er him sways.

To pause by rain-drenched earth beguiled,
Reflects upon the ghost and child.

Iron hinges yield a place within,
Absorbed by the tavern's raucous din
Will cleaves the dense tobacco's stench
Then several ales his palette quench.

Ere silver mourns a tot of rum
Will's mind and wit less taut become
Then obligation's heavy chain
No more his conscience seeks to strain.

He views with unpretentious eye
The drunken sons of revelry,
Well relieved of former nerves
The various types he now observes:-

Be lean and gaunt with hollow shirt
Imbibed with ample share of dirt,
Or waistcoat clad (of scarlet suede)
By corpulence more bulbous made,

Ale parlours no distinction show
To whomsoe'er should swell the flow,
All crease at humour's coarser vain
With oft told joke heard yet again.

Here many a joke Nick Spender makes
And many a round or gesture fakes,
Oft times withdrawn by false alarm
So never a crown should leave his palm.

While tousled Roland hogs the heat
Well anchored by his ample seat
Tobacco's wisps on mantles float
Newborn where hearthside smokers gloat.

And nimbler folk pass to and fro
To flick the orange candle glow
With tumblers raised their reeling forms
To a lesser brand of grace conforms.

Seen through the tainted azure haze
Lurks one of less gregarious ways,
Pale wrinkled hands in stealth immersed
Seldom bleed his leather purse.

Each visual image craves to thwart
The nobler mind's objective thought,
While yet each image starts to sway
To countenance the close of day.

Will bears the landlord's jovial mirth,
Procures a room for silver's worth,
Then faltering steps o'er landings creep,
Within the hour succumbs to sleep,
To dwell in dreams that rest nor solace keep.

***

When light transforms the hour where night has fled
And ragged dogs the fresh grey cobbles tread
And morning folk the cockerel strains nigh heard
Surmount the mundane tasks with cordial word,

Then shall men of fortune seize their wake
To full advantage of the dawn hours take.

And goes there one of steadfast true resolve
Pledged by his oath a mystery to solve.
Determined whatsoever be the cost
To compensate an unknown infant's loss.

Beyond the road upon a hill
Where gallows brace their cruel arm
With a task fulfilled hangs good Long Will,
May God protect his soul from harm.

Kip's Dream

I fall asleep and return to being my nine-year-old self, reliving adventures of my boyhood in kinetic transitions through various episodes, and encountering the focus of my fantasy make-believe world at the time:- The Centre of All Promise.

By the hearth of sweet elm burning
Cherishing the room around,
Sanctuarising in a string
Quartet's exquisite threads of sound,
Where my broader vision sees
The treasured objects in its frame
And finds the crystal-circled brandy
Takes its lustre from the flame
As smoke about the Turk's head curling
From the handled meerschaum born
Rises from the bowl unfurling
Where a rich tobacco's drawn

My repose by fortune blessed,
Now settled in its natural span,
Finds within contentments' rest
Rejuvenation of the man.

Yet as idle contemplation
Stays me in its comforts there
I am drawn by strange compulsion
From the velvet wing-backed chair,

Slowly rising, acting on
A hidden force that beckons me
To where a porcelain rests upon
The sideboard's dark mahogany,

Its polished surface now adorning
Purchased when I was a boy,
Once unwrapped on Christmas morning
When it gave Mum so much joy.

Here the object of my stare
Prolonged in its intensity,
Rendering me unaware
Of changes now surrounding me

Where just the china stays the same
While all else alters as a whole,
Permeating where a changing
Hearth's aroma turns to coal,

Summoning a well-remembered past
Emerging from the gloom
Where the light of flickering embers
Dances in a smaller room.

Here I survey the little space
In awe within its walls beguiled,
That familiar special place:
The house I lived in as a child.

Once more my focus rests upon
The china on its different shelf
Where the link to decades on
Is just the porcelain itself.

A door's ajar for me to creep
Into the tiny hallway there,
Mum and Dad will be asleep
And I must not traverse a stair

Nor cause a change by touch or feel
(In my new situation cast)
To any objects, dreamt or real,
Where I must not disturb the past,

But tentatively tread the floor
Where creaks the carpet-covered board,
Approaching the unlatched front door
That opens of its own accord,

And feel the chill about my face
As I embrace a vista bright
Where snowflakes every surface grace
To end their driftings through the night.

Here the amber lantern's glow
On winter's white is cast,
My leather tread that dints the snow's
A vision of the past,

Until more vivid comes the dream
When steps are crisp and sure,
In freezing aura now I seem
To be a child once more,

Who hears the 'hiss' where settles snow
On leaves in crystal air
And night's clear light its promise shows:
The slide at Laggan Square.

Enhanced the flakes about me where
I tread the virgin snow
Now drift across the street lamp sphere
To kiss the ice below

And settle in soft swirls
Along the surface of the slide
Whose darker course unfurls
Through silent white on either side.

Above the heavy sombre cloud
A fleeting moon appears,
How am I here in midnight's shroud?
(One of such tender years).

Enthralled when larger flakes appear
To spread snow's vista wide,
In savouring the atmosphere
I move towards the slide.

My weathered shoe's initial slip
That thwarts the start desired
In several strides provides the grip
To meet the pace required,

Then further to accelerate
Until a stance is set,
I overtake the swirling flakes
When ice and leather's met

In a sliding swerve, precarious, where
Kinetic soles are laid
And hurtle through the freezing air,
Red scarf and jacket splayed,

To glide beneath snow-laden bows'
Swift passing mantle stark,
The slide's reflective aspect now's
Absorbed into the dark,

Denying rationality
On which clear thought depends,
Can this just be as fantasy
The slide that never ends?

Or passes into dark abyss
Beyond the frozen street
Maintaining my momentum
With no ice beneath my feet?

Now weightless in the harsh night air
Propelled by mystic force
Through terrifying darkness
Where a nightmare runs its course

That finds me in a hostile place
(Illusive to the sight)
'Til sudden warmth assails my face
From distant source of light

Where I decelerate and fall
Towards the tunnel's end
And rays illuminate the cavern walls
As I descend,

To drift where wider spreads the light
Now brighter than before
And emerge into the sunlight
On the edge of North Town Moor,

Rejoicing in the freedom of a
Green and open space
Where my dream has skipped a season
Into summer's warm embrace,

That welcomes me from levity
To tread the level ground,
Becalmed within the fragrant foliage
Of a broad surround.

I stand where fears have come to naught
From cold transition, dark and strange,
Pausing to collect my thoughts,
Bewildered by the sudden change

And entered into balmy textures
Of a season's lush terrain
Where a world of great adventures
From my boyhood lives again.

In its draw I pause a while
Deliberating what to do,
Dev is waving from the stile
And Brian too comes into view.

Just as I'd taken to the slide
I once again self-motivate
And cross the field with eager stride
To where both friends and games await,

In some great drama to engage
With youthful creativity
And envy not those of our age
Who suffer from maturity.

Dev strikes the stance of Alan Ladd,
Imagined gun (he makes the sound)
I wouldn't normally be glad
To reel from shots and hit the ground

Or find such fun in being wronged
And wracked with final suffering
But this death from the gun's prolonged
By histrionic staggering.

I'll have to say I'm only winged
(delay the fall embarked upon)
Should negative reaction bring
I'll have the gall to carry on,

Until our mutual mirth dictates
Absurdity be put to bed,
For lack of props the game abates
To set upon our quest instead.

Near-normal dialogue ensues
And Brian says he's almost sure
(When pressed for all important news)
He's seen Red Devil on the moor.

Beyond the stile some eighty paces
Venturing forth our threesome team,
Striding north t'wards open spaces
Reach the bank to cross the stream.

Though Dev's suggestion merits 'Good'
The narrow bridge should caution urge,
The last time we played Robin Hood
Was when I ended up submerged.

The bridge we cannot circumvent
But at its centre halt our tracks,
Lingering here I'll be content
Observing newts and sticklebacks,

'Til uncharacteristically
We all curtail the verbal flow
And stand, transfixed, we silent three
To scrutinise the stream below.

Is it there? We can't be sure
Through softly flowing depths of green
The sinister dark predator,
Known just from hearsay, never seen,

'Til from our awestruck gazes freed
Beneath the sunbathed ripples bright
The dull green pike that cleaves the weed
In silent stealth has passed from sight.

Quick to share his observation
Dev extols the monster's strength,
Immediate exaggeration
Gives the pike some extra length.

It's all a sign we might suppose
And Brian's face assumes a scowl
"Before the day has reached its close
We'll see Black Devil on the prowl."

I'll not embrace uncertainty
That courts the mythological
Nor seek out proof, no guarantee
Supports assertions fanciful,

Our worlds of make-believe are as we choose,
Enshrouded in the wild expansive acres of the moor,
Beyond the stream and hawthorn ditch
Close-bordering the Cricket Pitch
We venture where eventually we'll reach Strand Castle door.

Erratic in our paths that each pursues,
Passing through the swathes of yellow cups that heed the breeze,
Their lacquered petals dancing over
Red milkwort and purple clover
Envying not our freedom where we travel as we please

Through descending mist that fading flora hides,
In broad expanse where my companions veer towards their ends,
And my involuntary course
Determined by compelling force
Seals my inability to save departing friends,

As drained of energy to faltering strides,
In my anxiety I breathe the heady moorland air,
Where through the mist the hollow tree,
Standing where it shouldn't be,
Appears a gnarled and twisted edifice to my despair,

A mocking silhouette that disappears,
Absorbed into an aura with its eerie shadows cast,
Where quests are rendered meaningless
And empty in the face of stress
To leave me just a memory of pals forever passed,

Where time is warped to magnify my fears
And make the minutes seem like hours or natural stanzas skip
'Til on a path that hosts my plight
(Strand Castle's grey facade in sight)
I hear Brian's voice come through the mist "Where did you get to Kip?"

A haze now rises from the clay-packed earth,
Revealing flecks of flora re-emerging into light
Where mist ascends through cobalt depth
To grant the sky unfettered breadth
And compliment my reassurance, all is put to right.

We three now reunited as from birth,
At ease to share the light that sees anxiety abate,
And though relief is on each face
We know the English don't embrace
Renewing cordial humour to restore the settled state.

Well known the light of youth is briefly shone,
And only treasured memories we save,
In anecdotal recall decades on
Will friendship's harvest live beyond the grave.

A sky transformed where breathes the darkened moor,
As fades a vista all-encompassing,
And taller now by far than seen before
Stands Strand Castle, stark and menacing.

Within its walls our destination reached,
Imagined foes just conjured visible,
Defending guards and iron portcullis breached,
Each deed of valour we've deemed credible.

Now stand we in an unfamiliar place
Where all's enlarged that measured reason jars,
A lofty tower compels each upturned face,
Its open reaching mantle greets the stars.

Two sets of spiral steps trace inner walls,
Each damp eroded grey stone bodes the threat of vertigo,
Yet still upon our venture bent
In simultaneous ascent
Dev and I assail their heights while Brian stands guard
below.

Higher on a ledge the night owl calls,
Questioning the wisdom of our quest-extended hour,
Where narrowing steps reduce the grip

"Don't go any higher Kip"
I slip and fall Dev's fading calling echoes through the tower,

Resounding with my desperate hollow cries,
The dreadful chorus heralding inevitable strife,
Yet seconds on my life's not ended
Where's the crash that fate intended
Now's prolonged the cloistered plunge to grant extended life.

'Though weird the fall still feared the great demise,
How can the distance on descent exceed that of ascent?
To harbour still the final dread
And how are steps now carpeted?
I crash into Dev's hallway with all crazed emotion spent.

The ghastly plummet lessened at its end,
Somehow I'm now enveloped in a cosy ambience,
Or in a dream within a dream
Aware things can't be as they seem
Yet feeling activated limbs regaining upright stance.

A message of false confidence to send,
Refocusing my swimming vision altered by the fall,
I see a children's gathering
Where Dev's great party's in full swing
As he descends the homely stairs and Brian smiles from the hall.

Where's hushed all tumult, just speaks Dev's dear mum:-
"It looks as though Kip's fallen from a castle in the sky"
The boys all chortle whereupon
Kind Mrs D. continues on:-
"But Johnny's a brave soldier and he's never known to cry."

Now all disperse each boisterous rival chum,
As through a haze a fairer vision feminine I see,
Her golden flowing locks caress
The white lace of her party dress
And where I stand she takes my hand "You've got to come with me."

My limbs reset in motion where her
soft request I heed
But in matters of this magnitude
the man should take the lead,

As though my thought's been read
she smiles before a word I've said,
The way that girls and women do
when they're two steps ahead.

Away from noise an empty room
provides secluded space,
Her softly spoken humour now
reflected in her face,

"No one at a party ever wears
a silly scarf,
You're so funny Johnny and you
always make me laugh."

Though she no longer holds my hand
her warmth is clear to see
(Backhanded though her welcome
compliment might seem to be).

It's not so clear what she's contrived
so must I read a clue?
I don't think we should cuddle girls
unless they want us to.

But men don't hesitate to kiss
the ladies on the screen
Why can't I emulate the cowboys
in the films I've seen?

With shyness cured and self-assurance
nothing interrupts,
God,
I'll hopefully be better at this
when we're both grown-ups.

Of course,
She might just want to talk on
railways, I'll need to explain,
When typically she'll think
a locomotive's called a train.

Oh well,
I'm drifting into a trance mode as I
question her intent,
While reflecting on the strangeness
of each recent mad event:-
The winter slide through dark transition
ending on the moor;
Cowboy games; the legendary pike
not seen before;
The loss, and subsequent return,
of friends so dear to me,
And even ghastly plummeting
has credibility,
But far less likely's when a girl
tells me that I should know
That her favourite locomotive is a
Castle 4-6-0.

Did she really say that
(is of me she making fun)?
Well,
Her beautiful conclusion
would suggest she might have done:-

"But best I'd love a carriage Johnny,
just with you and me,
That could whisk us on our holiday
to Weymouth by the sea."

Ah,
That lovely sentiment to me's
the best she could express,
I mean,
Too close to oil and metal things
would only spoil her dress.

She's read my mind again
and to its thought makes odd reply
"Not every engine's metal Johnny,
look up in the sky."

The darkness through an open window
challenges my sight,
Is finally the object of her guidance
brought to light?

My feet traverse a beige armchair
to tread the windowsill
Where all without in humid air's
unnaturally still

And soundless in its boundless breadth
as I now scan the view,
Pre-thunderous and motionless
save one cloud passing through.

Beyond the rooves there slowly moves
its apparition stark,
A locomotive formed of vapour
Tractioning the dark.

Above the silhouettes no metal form
its route could take,
Just visible the floating vapour
Coaches in its wake.

All trackless awesome spectres there
the laws of physics breach,
To course towards the West
across a northern starless reach,

And there (as though of me aware)
its presence to impose,
Beyond Hale's darkened field
the silent ghost-like image slows,

To hover in a stillness
set for stirrings of the night
Where issues thunder's rumble
from a distant flash of light,

Illuminating darkest Northern breadths
beyond the moor
To break the all-embracing calm
and turbulence ensure.

With thunder's louder rumblings now
rain rides a mounting breeze
In consort there to soak the ground
and animate the trees.

Here freed from its residual calm
Dev's garden patch receives,
With increasing wailing wind,
The wild erratic swirling leaves,

As flurries splash the panes
An open frame facilitates
My being drawn on to a ledge
The driven torrent saturates.

Now drenched and apprehensive
Where foreboding rules the head,
A slender distance from the room
Where manifest the dread,

I'm clinging to iron window frames
(Compelled the sideways glance)
Where horizontal curtains flail
In mad flamboyant dance.

Is all that's warm and welcoming
Now set to disappear?
A girl's 'the Centre of all Promise'
In that amber sphere.

Scarce audible her urgent voice
"It's time to say goodbye,"
Through a window metaphorical
Goes Mrs D's kind lie,
"But Johnny's a brave soldier and he's never known to cry."

Yet from that little girl's face
Does a kindness emanate?
Is she reluctant now
To use her power to devastate?

Or as from Helen's Troy
Must I now voyage through the night?
Is hers the face that launches mortals
Into skyward flight?

A lightning flash with thunder's crash
Tenfold the sound before,
And now I know that dreadful locomotive
Wields its draw,

Torrential hail where rails the gale
I can't maintain my grip,
All hoped-for promise won't prevail,
Feet on the wet sill slip.

I'm wrenched asunder flailing
From my rain-drenched sanctuary,
Now drawn towards that awesome train
Defying gravity.

All activated muscles share
My floundering 'til shoulders brace,
I'm swept aloft where moistured air
Bestows its harshness on the face
That's set towards the strange night train
Now forging West ahead of me
As over Brian's dark roof's maintained
My hurtling trajectory.

In chancing backward glance I find
I reached a terrifying height,
My dreamt-of girl I've left behind
Still waving from Dev's distant light,

Continues on my wild ascent
Where thunder compliments despair
'Til comes a hush – I've entered dense
Grey cloud where's less the rush of air,

From mist immersed where speed's increased
With every backward glance denied
I blast into a vast expanse
Of black where bright the stars preside,

Vivid here that locomotive's
Wild half profile just ahead,
Swirls of racing moon-bathed vapour
From its awesome spectre shed,

Enlarged by dire proximity
Great vapour driving wheels rotate,
As if to breach infinity
The speeding image penetrates
A sky where I still pace its climb
(The frantic traction drawn towards)
A freezing forearm locks on mine,
I reel exhausted – hauled aboard,

A half-transparent stoker there
In vapour swathes who shovels air
While faceless driver at the helm
In nebulous and fading realm
Could in a guise the reaper be
Determining my destiny
Approaching now some dreadful brink
With every image less distinct
Where sound of a rapid air-rush fades
And disappears each pale grey shade
From lightning's flash a second on
The locomotive ghost is gone.

As thunder rumblings fade away
Does darkness close my final day?
Have I now entered into death?
Was in the past my final breath?

Here in this terrifying silence
Runs the chill of empty dread,
Am I now trapped a consciousness,
In nothingness, if I am dead?

And was my end to travel on
That which reverts to former norm?
The Ghost of *The Bristolian*
That must return to iron form.

If I no longer here exist
Can be reversed outrageous fate
To predetermined course resist
And see restored my finite state?

Where now's reborn the vanished train
(That drew me into skyward strife)
To greet from colourless domain
The rich kaleidoscope of life.

Is never-dreamt-of silence endless?
I no longer see nor feel,
Emptiness is all-pervasive,
My bleak thoughts alone are real.

Darker seems this deeper sleep
Than any living mortal's known,
Life suspended seeks release
In gravity with feet on stone

To feel once more the sweet sensation
Of a breeze that drifts the rain,
Welcoming my liberation,
Finite life to thrive again.

From that blissful state's emergence
(As in birth's initial gasp)
Manifest in life's resurgence
Some new dawn's within my grasp,

Here relieved of my despairing,
Once again I breathe and live,
Englishness determining
Response that's undemonstrative.

I stand on a deserted platform's
Solid surface hankered for,
Lengths of shining steel on sleepers
Reach towards a Dorset shore.

Having weathered nightmare trials
With some new phase to undergo,
Never was a miserable
Drizzle ever welcomed so,

Dampening an empty station
Where chilled air embraces me,
Morning brings its grey salvation
Where through mist the sun I see,

Observing its pale shallow arc
From onset t'wards its end,
Even by my standards
I've gone into overpend.

Now approaching 'six' having languished in hours
I dwell on just minutes ahead,
Someone's taken the trouble to plant some flowers
On the platform at Maidenhead,

Where out to the West a Great Western Express
Could well be on its Paddington run,
Is by now *The Bristolian* down from the cutting
At Sonning approaching a 'ton'?

Where the driver and stoker int'ract as a team
Using levers and shovels unleashing the steam,
With swift action is traction maintained on the plate?
Does the stoker shift coal as a staggering rate?

Can the driver now see there's a station ahead
Where I stand on the platform at Maidenhead?
And observe at some distance the billows of smoke
As the Castle Class makes its ferocious approach,

Now racing The Gullet past signal and shed
The Bristolian nameplate can nearly be read
As coal to the fire the green boiler supplies
While the black frontal aspect increases in size

Now approaching the platform one hell of a lick
With each mad revolution the cylinders tick
Tick tick, tick tick, tick tick, tick tick,
Tick tick, tick tick, tick tick, tick tick,

Now to blast through the station fired thunderous black
With connecting rods racing devouring the track
Chocolate carriages flash:- tkd clack, tkd clack,
Tkd clack, tkd clack, tkd clack, tkd clack,

Dclack, it's gone (metal rattle and clack
Over gaps in the track) to Paddington,
It's gone where the racket and clatter goes on,
The Great Western Castle seven carriages long
Disappears in the distance (arrived and moved on)
Transformed to iron form *The Bristolian*,

And I amble a circle, it's still around 'six',
Hasn't taken that long my Bristolian fix.

So I saunter once more to embrace the hours
Yet dwell on the minute that's fled
And reflect on the Great Western culture that's ours
With its platform at Maidenhead

Where out on a bench with no locos in sight
My meandering settles to rest
And I savour the flowers in the evening light
With a breeze that now breathes from the West.

A breeze that leaves a coastal shore behind,
In just off-silent surges from the sea,
'Though drifting whispers aren't to me confined,
Subjectively their message rests with me,

Where wordless beckoning each breath conveys
And triggers pictures of a different sort
For memories of Weymouth holidays
To settle into meditative thought

On how we comprehend a spoken word,
Who's construct's in the future or the past,
A present with no time-width seems absurd,
So recall any instant must outlast

And lengthen should a sentence breach the ear
Through soporific barrier to the brain,
Here manifest Mum's anxious voice I hear:-
"Come on John, rouse yourself, we'll miss the train".

Somnambulance to urgency gives way,
Initial slow reaction leads to action on the call,
Through smoke and issuing steam I see
A locomotive sedentary
But why a mighty shining King Class not a dull black Hall?

I momentarily my dash delay,
To gaze on its magnificence at this eleventh hour,
Where copper rims the funnels heat
And dark green iron the smoke box meet
The curving blackened steam pipe shoulders hold releasing power,

To grant me time to carriages appraise,
That stretch the empty platform's length where nearer's heard Mum's voice,
We board and walk a corridor
To operate a sliding door
Compartments empty guarantee the luxury of choice.

One small prerequisite of holidays,
Now two compartments having passed we choose a third instead,
With leather case on netting rack
I smile at Mum and she smiles back,
Pleased for me to sit the right way round and face ahead.

Aware that what seems ours is there for all,
A railway carriage's seclusion may just last a day,
I survey all compartment fixtures,
Either side the landscape pictures
Never doing justice to the scenes that they portray.

A sudden jolt inaugurates the haul,
The platform's now receding to the sound of tractioning steam,
But why was there no whistle blown?
No slamming doors we've always known?
Events unfolding raise the question 'are things as they seem?'

Yet visually normality obtains,
And rhythmically predictable's the King's release of power:-
Four funnels chuffs to each rotation,
Two'll maintain acceleration,
Soon will single rhythmic ticks hold eighty miles per hour,

Increasing as our train momentum gains,
As seemingly a scheduled stop's been prematurely reached,
Now heightening our speed sensation
Hammering through Twyford Station
On to Sonning Cutting where a hundred could be breached.

But how can we by now have come this far?
It's more than clear to me that speed and distance don't relate,
Now Wiltshire's White Horse Hills are spreading,
How can we have missed out Reading?
Fast though over eighty feels it doesn't quite equate.

Mum looks to be at one with how things are
(Contrasting with my deep unease, remaining calm and still)
I view a slowly moving sky
With closer foliage racing by
Bemused by her endearing words:- "Look at that lovely hill."

With nature's undulations all observed,
Where Wiltshire's golden fields recede and greener Dorset calls,
Any second hollow sounds
Will penetrate its gentler downs
We're funnelled through a sudden tunnel's racing blackened walls.

To find me by the darkness more unnerved,
Where making sense of these events won't just depend on sight,
Now focused on the sliding door
A figure in the corridor's
Illuminated briefly by the flickering carriage light.

Revealed th'angelic face I recognise,
I gain my feet with boyhood passion triggered once again,
A fleeting glimpse showed clearly my
Sweet dreamt-of girl who'd waved goodbye
Now vanished, moving relatively faster than the train.

Short-lived elation borne of my surprise,
A light no longer flickers where the dark envelops all,
I now no speed sensation feel
Nor hear the sound of wheels on steel
A mirror there before me shows a dark Edwardian hall-

-way where my barely visible reflection registers the stare
That ascertains to whom belong the threads of silver hair,
My dear Aunt Lily stands with Mum enhanced by
candlelight,
How can the rational mind deny the evidence of sight?

Or question the Victorian rug on tiles beneath my feet,
Horlor's painting by the hall stand? Transformation's now
complete.
My aunt's embracing Mum as though protecting her from
harm
(It's just how women are, you often see them arm in arm).

She flicks a switch for instant light that forty watts affords
To illuminate the cosy hallway we've been drawn towards
And having changed a bulb proceeds to snuff the candle
out,
Yet 'til she speaks all I've perceived as real must be in doubt:-

"It's wonderful to see you, have you taxied from the town?
Look at you now growing up, how was your journey down?"

Had I, at this juncture (having placed our leather case)
Stood and looked into my dear Aunt Lily's lovely face
And told her I had dreamt that I was seventy before
Embarking on a slide that detoured onto North Town Moor,
And met with Dev and Brian before a dire unscheduled fall
Had rendered me bewildered but not really hurt at all
Where I'd managed to regain my feet when unexpectedly
A little girl had offered help and redirected me
To an overhead conveyance where I'd dreamt that I was dead
Before meeting up with Mum to catch the train from Maidenhead,
Then emphasised our frantic journey hadn't taken long,
She'd never have believed me, then again I could be wrong.

As it was Mum had replied on how our trip began:-
A taxi? Followed by the train ride? All had gone to plan?
How finally we'd been conveyed I'd failed to quite take in,
Now Aunt Lily's underway with Weymouth's bulletin:-

"The works proposed at Bowlees Cove…" had suffered some delay,
Postponing any detrimental change to Weymouth Bay,

My grandma, down from Holyport, and Joy my cousin too
Had called on Tilly on their way to Swanage passing through,

The floral clock had looked a picture earlier in the year
And a talent competition had been held on Weymouth Pier.

No mention of the hook-nosed rogue I've disliked all my life-
(The repellent red-apparelled misfit bullying his wife)
Still with its visual fascination, that I understand
(The brightly coloured striped theatre standing on the sand).

The donkeys do, by contrast, get a mention here, besides,
They'll look to be well cared for giving children seaside rides,

Nearby a sculptor's crystallised envisaged images,
Not forgetting Lily's father's plaque on Weymouth Harbour Bridge.

Are all the things my aunt's describing fast approaching ten?
The way that women natter on is quite unlike the men,
Who always know 'some idiot' (too bumptious like as not)
Who've come unstuck, got made redundant, 'thought they knew the lot'.

Untypical is Uncle Stan, whom we shall shortly see,
He'll be there in the parlour at his desk or drinking tea,
And greet me as I enter, where before I get to speak,
He'll inform me he's enrolled me in a school for one whole week,

Then ask for some 'impressions' of the characters I know
(Al Read or some comedian we've heard on radio).
Impersonations often thrive on spontaneity,
My inhibition could deny rendition's accuracy.

We've entered, Stanley's in his chair where upwards curls the smoke,
I think the school-enrolment scare was only last year's joke,
A non-inclusive grown-up's conversation will ensue
As no impersonation's been requested hitherto.

I opt for silent exit with our precious leather case,
Predictably the treasures of the hallway still in place,
Accustomed though I am to transformation's every claim,
As recently there's been no guarantee things stay the same.

To reach the bedroom here entails one-eighty in the hall,
A narrow carpet's held by stair rails, thirteen stairs in all,
Youth needs no help from that which seeks to justify its role
The hand-supporting bannister that compliments the whole,

And guides me over upper landing's undulating floor,
My left hand turns the handle of a panelled bedroom door,

To enter in a silent and secluded sanctuary,
A room that's reassuringly unchanged,
With all familiar furniture and objects that I see
Discerningly and carefully arranged,

Where dominates a wardrobe with its mirrors in the doors,
A scuttle that's exclusively for coal,
And on the polished surface of a Georgian chest of drawers
A blue and white Victorian jug and bowl.

I place the case to circumnavigate the made-up bed,
Through open windows breathes the sweet sea air,
I shed the shoes, a moonlit pillow's where I rest my head
With both hands held behind dishevelled hair.

The ceiling's mundane shade's bereft of merit here I see,
Not so the cord-hung pictures on the walls,
Revealing each arrested time in perpetuity,
A photograph a faded past recalls.

I should repair downstairs, they'll be aware I've not returned,
In dwelling on my long-held view we're moulded at our birth
I question whether 'All should for my welfare be concerned'
Is an only child's obsession with inflated sense of worth,

Then contemplate a further question entering my mind
That asks on what, importantly, a man's worth should depend?
It must be on the things he does, not clothes of any kind,
Not even coloured braces, leather fastenings at each end.

My simple analytical deliberations fade as I unwind
And close my eyes as holiday's anticipated images appear,
To conjure at the close of day a melancholic picture in the mind
Where light reflects on sad dark sea that laps the iron uprights
of the pier.

I must have slumbered, unaware, with sleep's nostalgic pictures in my head,
As now our case has been removed, Mum's laid my pyjamas neatly on a chair,
I slowly rouse, my feet re-occupy the waiting shoes beside the bed,
I've never in the past within these walls of such a silence been aware.

Now every object in the room the sparsity of faded moonlight shares,
I creep towards the door (that's just ajar) as if in answer to a call,
Aunt Lily's left a light on in the hallway at the bottom of the stairs,
The landing's opposite direction beckons where the dark envelops all.

Here all who sleep behind closed bedroom doors can only sojourn in their dreams,
While, with all faculties prevailing, man has self-accountability
And need not heed a call unknown that's beckoning, compelling though it seems,
Yet I cannot return to bed 'til satisfied's my curiosity.

The landing should to me be all familiar from our holidays before,
Instead it's cloaked in almost total darkness with its boundaries unclear
Where's ushered in an outside breeze as I traverse its unlit corridor,
Cautiously advancing, barely audible some distant sounds I hear.

Continuing my venturing it's clear a transformation's taking place,
The corridor's extending, visual images now marry with the sounds,
I'm unaware of total distance covered, salt sea air assails my face,
I'm walking on an elevated area the dark night sea surrounds.

Here all about's evolving and with every strange and recent change accords,
Finding I'm on Weymouth Pier from past encounters can't provide surprise
Where underfoot the landing rug has given way to damp well-trodden boards
And that sad sea I'd visualised I view below with conscious open eyes,

And overlook the weathered iron stanchions of the pier, then turn away
To face towards a brightly lit oasis that I take in at a glance,
Alfresco sounds orchestral emanate from eight musicians where they play
And pretty ladies on a stage arrest my full attention as they dance.

I'm readily adjusting to an altered state, now having come this far,
And watch the ladies in a dance that must from some unfolding story stem,
They always love to twirl about and demonstrate how feminine they are,
In films I've seen they love to be kissed just as much as men love kissing them.

As yet there are no men on stage, they could be in the story later on,
I walk to stand behind the little audience more senior in years,
Whose carefree youthful escapades in halcyon days might well have come and gone,
While I, with all my life ahead, am still beset with adolescent fears,

Now standing with the sense that this could be a closing episode on stage,
It can't have been a part of some long drama, just an isolated scene,
The audience is clapping and the ladies and musicians all engage,
It seems to me the things that come about are almost always unforeseen.

One certainty's that every adult has a different walk they don't disguise,
And all who now are standing shortly demonstrate this unique faculty,
Not looking where they're going could be just a trait in which some specialise,
Or am I being closely passed by taller folk who've failed to notice me?

The trouble is with being young we're mostly governed, seldom at the helm,
And here a lack of cognizance would mark some grown-ups' exits from the pier
Who've ambled in proximity with nonchalant approach to overwhelm,
Leaving me to contemplate a vital question: Am I really here?

Where almost all have left the pier and night its tranquil atmosphere retains,
With chattering's diminished leaving just the lonely whispers of the sea,
And as the last of adults pass a solitary figure there remains,
Come softly-spoken tones familiar, "Hello Kip, I knew where you would be."

My expectation's never made provision for the vision that I see,
Nor dared to entertain the possibility of such a welcome sight,
Yet all elation's tempered as I comprehend her vulnerability,
She mustn't think that she can roam around alone unchaperoned at night.

I'm finally directional, no intervening change must hold the sway,
The lost (referred to) 'silly scarf' I can't provide, so simply take her hand,
My jacket would afford her warmth had I not shed it earlier in the day,
I'll settle for our exiting the pier descending steps to Weymouth sand,

Traversing first the weathered boards approaching stanchion's broader westward view,
And overlooking harbour lights, beyond dark Portland shines the midnight star,
Her unexpected question, as I'm entering the realms of déjà vu,
Comes knowingly and softly spoken "Have you figured out, Kip, where you are?"

I need not fully comprehend, but in some natural ordered outcome trust,
A man, in acting as he can, endeavours to each situation save,
So in the end when good prevails he tips the scales to save the girl and must
Adopt, as Anglo heroes in adventure tales, the mindset of the brave.

We tread descending steps where spreads the sand beneath our feet
And walk its damper texture where the land and ocean meet
As soft each surge of moonlit surf reflects along the shore
A shadow looms before us I've imagined here before.

Within that dark theatre where the puppets rest their heads
The buckled supine misfit never red apparel sheds,
I steer to veer and could be near the donkeys where they sleep,
The sculptor's crafted artistry its visual secrets keep.

From steps ascended harbour bridge,
Past Eustace plaque an unenvisaged
Heightened sense of déjà vu
In passing Rodwell Avenue.

Where never was before a field
A moonlit vista's here revealed
Descending in its broader reach
To pebbled breadth of Chesil Beach

Here on its dark Atlantic side
The wilder night's advancing tide.

Released a hand towards the sea;
Revived increased anxiety;
Retained my clear protective pledge
She mustn't veer too near the edge

Where falls the beach to slide the feet
That could deny our swift retreat.

The ocean, as if drawing breath
On shingles rushing threatens death,
I make a dash to grab her arm
To drag her back away from harm,
As shining pebbles swallow feet
The sea completes its harsh retreat
Now heaving from some dreadful depth
Accumulating surf-capped breath
And bearing down as still we slide
(The saturating crashing tide)
With sudden blockage of the ears
Endorsed the claustrophobic fears,
Submersed we now where all that's seen
Is hostile brine of darkest green,
Immersed as in some Chesil hell
(The last ordeal that won't end well)
Still held her arm that draws me down,
Is it so easy now to drown?
Where resignation mustn't reign
As drawn to Davy Jone's domain,
In swirling darkness still submerged
The current turns; reversed the surge,
Extended reach secures my grasp,
The surface reached; procured the gasp,

A moon-enhanced advancing wave
Might yet the situation save,
We're half-submersed within its bore
In surging surf towards the shore,
As if delivered from hell's place
By some great overseeing grace.
The rushing foam assails the beach
To drench the stones within our reach,
We're scrambling back where rides the spray
"It's all right Kip, I'll be OK."
Still held her arm to higher ground
As fade all ocean sounds around
Save shifting shingle here intent
On halving progress of ascent
While still retained through hostile night
Her hand 'til gained some greater height
And distant surf conveys to me
Its closing message from the sea.

Life gave no sweeter shared relief
Than 'saved the girl' and 'spared the grief'.

Together still we climb the hill
As daylight breaks on Portland Bill.
Here where dawns the fresh new day
Some spirit in me drifts away,
Alone to face the tidal 'Race'
(An adult to a future place)

Invisible I turn to stand
And see two children, hand in hand,
And know before me there I see
The nine-year-old I used to be
Who from the pier has taken care
Of his imagined girlfriend there,
So as all other life unfolds
Remains their world of nine-year-olds.

I turn once more towards the sea,
The decades hence that beckon me,
Where recollections still inspire,
The rising sun a fading fire.

By the hearth of elm log embers
Now my dream's expired at last
I dwell on times dreamt or remembered
From a treasured boyhood past.